Little Red's Lost Cap

Written by Fiona Undrill

Illustrated by Eugenia Nobati

Collins

One spring, Little Red went up to the top of the steep rocks.

She was not afraid – until a gust of wind lifted off her cap.

Little Red ran back down the steep rocks in tears.

"I lost my scarlet cap!" she wept.

"Hush, my sweet darling!" Mum said. "You can have my smart black cap."

Little Red did *not* like the cap.
She started moaning.

Stop complaining!

"It hurts!" Little Red burst out.
"The strap under my chin is too tight!"

Frowning and groaning, Little Red went out in the smart black cap.

Little Green and his troop snorted.
"What a plain cap!" he said.
"It's not bright!"

A sudden *swoop* of wind lifted off
Little Green's cap.

One by one, all of the bright caps floated off in the wind.

The wind was howling! The troop all needed caps with straps.

All the caps with straps were smart black ones. Just like Little Red's.

How is Little Red feeling?

After reading

Letters and Sounds: Phase 4

Word count: 159

Focus on adjacent consonants with long vowel phonemes, e.g. *sweet*.

Common exception words: do, he, my, of, to, the, no, I, all, by, she, was, you, said, have, like, were, little, one, out, what

Curriculum links: Art and design; Science: Animals including humans

National Curriculum learning objectives: Reading/word reading: apply phonic knowledge and skills as the route to decode words; read accurately by blending sounds in unfamiliar words containing GPCs that have been taught; read common exception words, noting unusual correspondences between spelling and sound and where these occur in the word; Reading/comprehension: understand both the books they can already read accurately and fluently and those they listen to by making inferences on the basis of what is being said and done

Developing fluency

- Read the book together with your child, using different voices for Little Red, Mum and Little Green.

- Demonstrate how to add emphasis to the words in italics on pages 6 and 10.

Phonic practice

- Focus on the long vowel sounds in words with adjacent consonants.

- Point to **steep** on page 2. Ask your child to sound out and blend. (s/t/ee/p)

- Ask your child to sound out and blend these words, identifying the letters that make the long vowel sound:

    sw**oo**p   sc**ar**let   gr**oa**ning   sn**or**ted   br**igh**t   compl**ai**ning

Extending vocabulary

- Ask your child to suggest synonyms (words with a similar meaning) for these words. Ask them to check their ideas work in the sentence.

    page 3: **afraid** (*scared, frightened*)   page 5: **sweet** (*lovely, dearest*)

    page 7: **burst** (*blurted, shouted*)   page 9: **plain** (*dull, colourless*)